Contents

Abstract

Since the early 1990s the DPRK has faced a prolonged period of adversity resulting from a combination of natural catastrophes and failed state policies. The fall of the Soviet Union in 1991 and the death of Kim-Il Sung in 1994, provoked many acrimonious debates among experts over when North Korea (NK) will cease to exist. The famine in 1997, claiming millions of lives, as well as devastating floods in 2007, have perpetuated these discussions, making the prospect for a collapse perhaps greater now than in any time in its history. Based on the German reunification model in the early 1990s, many studies have focused on what a DPRK collapse would mean to the region, to include the future of a unified Korea. While the main emphasis of these works is typically reunification, this research paper spotlights the concept of regional multilateralism in managing a DPRK collapse.

In doing so, this study sets out to address the following questions: First, why is multilateral engagement so difficult to execute in Northeast Asia, and what are the dynamics involved? Second, does a collapse of the DPRK government necessarily result in immediate reunification, and how does this affect the application of multilateralism? Finally, what are the implications to U.S. interests in the region, and what recommended courses should it consider?

This paper begins with a twentieth century look at multilateralism in East Asia by examining a wealth of expert historical and contemporary analysis. Next, a potential multilateral framework is presented with an analysis of the associated benefits and complexities related to the concept. The key issue of reunification is also revealed, specifically whether a DPRK government collapse would equal immediate reunification. Finally, this study concludes with a look at the implications of using multilateralism in dealing with this crisis to future U.S. interests in Northeast Asia.

I. Introduction/Assumptions

In late 2008, unconfirmed reports from multiple international news agencies stated the likelihood that DPRK leader Kim Jong-Il (KJI) had suffered a stroke and undergone possible brain surgery.[1] The last confirmed instance of a public appearance by KJI was on 25 April 2008, when he headed the 75th anniversary celebration of the North Korean People's Army in Pyongyang.[2] Due to the poor state of NK, coupled with the lack of a known successor, the possibility of a collapse of the DPRK government exists, resulting in a humanitarian crisis as well as the prospect of immediate absorption into the Republic of Korea (ROK).[3] A recent study by the Council on Foreign Relations (CFR) stated that in addition to immense economic costs, the U.S. and its allies would have to deploy up to 460,000 troops to NK to stabilize the country.[4] The need for the U.S. to consider a regional multilateral framework may be greater now than at any previous time, to include the Korean War.

In order to proceed with this research, certain assumptions had to be made, particularly regarding what a DPRK government collapse would entail. The death of KJI with no known successor, would likely result in a government collapse, because of the totalitarian nature of the regime, coupled with the cult of personality surrounding the Kim family.[5] Additionally, the closed nature of the society would prevent word of collapse from spreading immediately. A self-proclaimed leader would likely emerge; however, the absence of an indentified successor may cause the legitimacy of the government to be called into question, resulting in a high risk to the breakdown of internal security. The chance for a humanitarian crisis is high throughout this period, with the potential of mass refugee flows into neighboring countries (People's Republic of China (PRC), Russia and the ROK). This scenario would slowly unfold over a period of weeks, allowing external powers to assess the situation, as well as conceive a plan of action.

1

II. Background: A Brief Look at Multilateralism in Northeast Asia

Multilateralism, defined as a process or framework used by a group of nations to discuss and resolve issues of an international nature, is not an inherent concept in Northeast Asia. While there is no definitive set of reasons for this lack of cooperation or integration, competing rivalries for regional dominance between China, Japan and Russia, with Korea at the center, are undisputedly major contributing factors.[6] The years following World War II (WWII) offer perhaps a microcosm of the struggles within Northeast Asia regarding multilateralism. Kent E. Calder, Director of the Reischauer Center for East Asian Studies, describes the Korean War and the 1997 Asian Financial Crisis as critical junctures affecting the emergence of multilateralism in Northeast Asia in the twentieth century.[7]

Following the fall of China to communist forces in 1949, the Pacific Pact concept was adopted as a mechanism to balance the perceived threat posed by China. The earliest proponents of this concept included the Philippines, South Korea, and Taiwan. Just as NATO was established in April that same year to contain the Soviet Union, the Pacific Pact was viewed as an Asian version to contain communist forces in China. The relative weakness of the Asian allies likely made a collective security option in Asia less attractive to the U.S. than in Europe; however, in 1951 a proposed draft was eventually developed within the U.S. government.[8] Still, contentious issues such as bilateral agreements over basing rights in Japan and Chinese intervention in the Korean War led the U.S. away from adopting such a pact.[9] In the end, the U.S. saw few benefits to multilateralism in the Pacific, when compared to potential costs and obligations. As a result, the Pacific Pact concept was abandoned in favor of multiple bilateral agreements between Pacific partners with the U.S. at the center. This "hub and spoke" method, better known as the San Francisco System of bilateral agreements, dominates today as the primary policy mechanism in East Asia.[10]

While the U.S.-led San Francisco bilateral system continues to predominate most of the region, international and regional forces such as globalization and the 1997 Asian Financial Crisis have pushed the region into greater economic integration.[11] The trauma of the 1997crisis appeared to spur national governments to adopt regional multilateral mechanisms in order to deal with or avoid similar events in the future. According to Calder's study, before the 1997 crisis, the countries of Asia were tied together in a loose, network style of regionalism. However, in the aftermath, regional powers such as China began promoting more multilateral engagement, culminating in the May 2000 Chiang Mai Initiative.[12] A slow move toward regional economic integration has continued since; however, there have been very few broad multilateral institutions that have gained traction.

In the southeast, the three most prominent broad multilateral institutions to gain a durable foothold in Asia are the Association of Southeast Asian Nations (ASEAN), the Asia-Pacific Economic Cooperation (APEC), and the Asia Cooperation Dialogue (ACD). ASEAN has also sprouted offshoots such as the ASEAN+3, the Asia-Europe Meeting (ASEM), the ASEAN Post-Ministerial Conferences (PMC), and the ASEAN Regional Forum (ARF).[13] While Northeast Asian countries actively participate in some of these forums, there are currently no official multilateral organizations established in their respective region. The Northeast Asia Cooperation Dialogue (NEACD) and the Northeast Asia Peace and Security Mechanism (NEAPSM) are unofficial groups involving the U.S., China, Japan, NK, the ROK, and Russia. Academic experts from these countries meet, separated from any official government positions, and discuss topics such as security policy, counterterrorism measures, and the Korean peninsula situation.[14] The Six-Party Talks (6PT) emerged in 2003 as a framework focused on resolving the dilemma over

NK's nuclear program.[15] This forum, still in existence, continues to meet (the last meeting was in June 2008), but has yet to broker a permanent resolution.

Despite these struggles, there are a number of potential benefits associated with pursuing multilateral engagement, particularly in the event of a NK collapse. The following section will address a few of these.

III. The Impetus behind Multilateralism

One of the leading advantages of multilateralism is its ability address concerns among regional and international partners, as well as potentially establishes the foundation to deal with future challenges. This policy option considers the sweeping issues related to a DPRK collapse and the vast resource requirements to address it. Multilateralism is arguably the best mechanism to effectively address the massive cost and burden sharing associated with stabilization and/or any future reunification of the two Koreas. While the ROK would ultimately be the most affected by this crisis, China, Japan, the U.S. and Russia also maintain a vested interest in the future of the peninsula, and should be included in any regional forum. Each of these nations shares a common interest in a socially stable and economically prosperous Korea. Additionally, they possess a special capacity to contribute to particular issues, to include refugee flows, energy assistance, political influence, and foreign direct investment.

Perhaps even more than the current "hub and spoke" method, multilateralism would strengthen the legitimacy of the U.S. role by projecting it as a unifier of regional interests rather than imposing its will to satisfy its own interests.[16] A concerted effort would increase the chances for quicker stabilization, allowing the ROK the opportunity to determine the extent of any future integration or reunification on its own terms, through gradual political and economic reforms.[17]

The reunification between East Germany (GDR) and West Germany (FRG) is a popular model among many academics to forecast the future of the peninsula resulting from any form of collapse of the DPRK.[18] While some similarities may exist in the two cases, the differences, particularly social and economic, are the most daunting. Korean expert Marcus Noland in his, *Economic Strategies for Reunification*, compares the DPRK and the GDR. The DPRK is much larger and poorer than the GDR was upon reunification, as well as being a more closed society, making the population's adjustment more difficult.[19] Additionally, the economy of the ROK is approximately 25 times larger than NK's compared to a smaller difference in gross domestic products of the FRG and GDR upon reunification.[20] This significant disparity underscores the need for a collective contribution in terms of capital and human effort in alleviating the repercussions of a collapse, regardless of the road to integration the ROK chooses to take.

With all the appeal that multilateralism may possess, there is equally a complex array of dynamics that make its successful application difficult to achieve. How do multiple countries with conflicting interests and agendas come to a mutually acceptable framework, and how would such a forum look?

IV: How to Get There—The Complexity of Multilateralism

The difficulty of multilateralism in Northeast Asia owes much of its cause to deep-rooted animosities among the regional powers as a result of persistent war and conquest. Throughout history, the Korean peninsula has long been the crossroads between China, Japan, Russia, and the U.S.; regarded by all as a launching point to shape influence in the region.[21] While the

United Nations (U.N.) has been involved in Korea from the days preceding the Korean War to today, regional multilateral forums have been unable to gain a permanent foothold. The first involvement by the U.N. regarding the "Korean question" occurred on 17 September 1945, when the U.N. General Assembly was called to settle a dispute between the U.S. and the Soviet Union regarding the establishment of a provisional government in Korea.[22] Ultimately, this disagreement was unresolved, leading to the division of Korea along the 38th parallel. This separation following 1945 has sustained the complex range of interests upsetting the foundation of an effective regional multilateral program.[23]

In 2003, the establishment of the 6PT framework was a step in the right direction toward laying the foundation for an enduring multilateral regional structure. As an addition, on September 19, 2005, a Joint Statement outlined principles referencing new "ways and means for promoting security cooperation in Northeast Asia" resulting in the creation of the Northeast Asia Peace and Security Mechanism (NEAPSM)[24] The focus on dialogue related to Northeast Asia security, especially regarding the state of NK, makes the NEAPSM a potentially viable option in dealing with a DPRK collapse.

Under this framework, the ROK would likely take the lead as well as carry the majority of responsibility in stabilization. During this time, it's crucial that any operation or aid provided to NK have a "ROK face" associated with it in order to ensure regional legitimacy and enhance the chances for an enduring peace. Additionally, continued support to this process by the U.N. provides an umbrella of international legitimacy important for long-term success. Organizations such as the U.N. High Commissioner for Refugees (UNHCR) and the International Atomic Energy Agency (IAEA) are just two examples of many U.N. entities that will have a significant role in assisting with numerous issues, ranging from humanitarian assistance to securing and controlling weapons of mass destruction (WMD).

Complexities, however, associated with the U.N. and the success of any proposed NEAPSM framework are revealing. Chapter V of the U.N. Charter lays out the structure of the Security Council (UNSC). Of the fifteen members, five possess permanent status with the power to veto any resolution.[25] Of these five permanent members, three (China, Russia, and U.S.) are also participants within the proposed NEAPSM framework. China or Russia could use the UNSC to contain or thwart a U.S. agenda resulting in friction or "watered down" strategies not conducive to U.S. or ROK interests.[26] A high degree of diplomatic acumen will be required to mitigate these potential challenges. In order for either the U.N. or the NEAPSM to succeed, some form of consensus will be required among these three nations. The key is to find common ground regarding the future of Korea (in support of the ROK) in order to proceed with this framework. Therefore, it's imperative to briefly exam the interests of these nations, particularly through the lenses of security, stability, and regional influence. Though Japan, Russia, China, and the ROK will be the primary participants covered in this section, the U.S. will be discussed in greater detail under Section VI: Implications to the U.S.

Attitudes regarding the future of Korea appear to be the most persistent and complex among regional powers. While reunification due to a NK collapse is widely accepted as the most likely scenario, doubts over the aspirations of a united Korea incline most regional members to favor maintaining two separate Koreas over reunification.[27] Maintaining regional security and stability is paramount, with any significant risk to normalcy sparking major concerns from of all members. The absence of strategic understandings on a range of issues to include WMD assets, deployment of U.S. forces north of the 38th parallel, humanitarian issues as well as border controls stemming from refugees, may lead more to conflict than cooperation, unless a multilateral dialogue begins early and becomes continuous.[28]

For Japan, the 1953 armistice has ensured that both Koreas focus a majority of their attention one one another rather than Tokyo.[29] For this reason, Japan would likely have the most to fear from a unified Korea, and would possibly be in favor of maintaining a separate NK in event of a collapse. Japan policy expert Hideki Yamaji suggests the best way to procure Japanese involvement in a regional framework is to maintain assurances of a separate bilateral alliance with the U.S.[30] Any potential withdrawal of U.S. forces from Korea following reunification, without reinforcing its posture in Japan, may force Tokyo to consider expanding its military, thus inciting a security dilemma in the region.

Russia's security concerns stem mostly from past border disputes with China and conflict with Japan over the Kurile Islands.[31] Since the fall of the Soviet Union, Russia's influence in the region has decreased considerably. However, as a permanent member of the UNSC, Russia's interests must be taken into consideration. Additionally, its geographic proximity coupled with concerns over U.S. proposed missile defense plans in the region give Russia grounds for close involvement in the future of Korea. As with all members, strategic interests such as economic development after stabilization will provide incentive for cooperation. Overall, stability free of control by any one regional power will likely favor Russia the most, regardless if Korea becomes unified or remains divided.[32]

Next to the ROK, China arguably views the stability and future of NK with the greatest interest. According to a 2002 study, there are two main interests driving China's security policy in the Asia-Pacific: economic development and achievement of great power status.[33] The separation of the two Koreas, with NK acting as a buffer zone from the U.S, has enabled China to focus on economic growth and military modernization. While in the long-term, a unified

Korea may offer economic stimulus to the region, the fears of a nuclear capable Korea closely allied with the U.S. may cause China to pursue "loose diplomatic coordination" with regional members, rather than promoting full cooperation and transparency.[34] Overall, China's response to a collapse is largely an unknown, representing a potential "wild card" in any collective response proposal.[35] Its role and cooperation may largely be determined by its perception of other regional member's interests, particularly the U.S.

The interests of the ROK in the collapse of NK are fairly apparent and should drive the agenda of the regional framework. Reunification is undisputedly a long-term objective of the ROK, and has been since the Korean War. However, under ROK policy, a phased process of reunification is preferred on the basis "of building a single Korean national community rooted in the values of freedom and democracy."[36] While a collapse may mark the end of a sixty-year military threat to the ROK, the list of emerging issues already discussed will be enormous. Chief among these concerns focusing on potential integration is *how* reunification should occur.

V. Does Collapse Equal Reunification? An Alternative Look

Most books focused on the reunification of Korea include a section comparing the different scenarios in which reunification may occur.[37] These scenarios usually range from a "soft landing" scenario, in which both sides amicably agree to gradual integration, to a "hard landing" scenario that occurs in the wake of conflict or a collapse.[38] In the case of a "hard landing" scenario, the common assumption is that the collapse of the DPRK will mean immediate reunification, similar to East and West Germany in 1990. This argument claims that once the perimeter of the closed North Korean society is breached, and the populace realizes the disparate living conditions, they will flood to South Korea looking for salvation. However,

9

depending on the degree and pervasiveness of a collapse, a timely effort on the part of the NEAPSM regional forum could afford the ROK other options. While reunification continues as a major policy objective of the ROK, the pace at which it happens is open to debate.[39] Due to the economic, social, and cultural divides separating the two Koreas, the daunting specter of immediate absorption may push the ROK to adopt an alternative option: confederation.

The idea of a Korean confederation is hardly a new concept. Contrary to its previous approach of reunification through revolution, NK has been espousing its desire for a confederation as a necessary and logical step toward reunification since 1960.[40] Kim Il-Sung spoke of a confederal structure that would "maintain the present different political systems of the North and South."[41] In October 1980, NK proposed the founding of the Democratic Confederal Republic of Korea as the ultimate form of a unified state. It claimed to take on the feature of "one nation, one state, two systems, and two regional governments."[42] The most recent statement regarding a confederation occurred in May 1998, when a DPRK spokesman argued that a proposed confederation between the two Koreas would require guarantees of protection by both sides to remain autonomous and on equal footing.[43] However, according to author Selig Harrison in his book *Korean Endgame: A Strategy for Reunification and U.S. Disengagement*, the root of the problem between North and South has centered on the issue of representation. South Korea has a much bigger population than the North, approximately 46 million compared to 25 million.[44] The ROK government promotes free legislative elections in both the North and South that would likely result in a South-dominated legislature. In turn, this would require the North to change its political system before any movement toward reunification could commence.[45] Consequently, the gridlock over this issue evaporated any hopes between the governments of forming a confederation as a first step toward reunification.

The collapse of the DPRK government; however, could create an environment conducive for both sides to revisit this path. If the ROK views an immediate absorption as potentially destabilizing to its institutional and social structure, it may be more receptive to adopting measures to slow the process. In his book, Harrison discusses a thesis by sociologist Roy R. Grinker over a proposal for a loose confederation or "Korean Commonwealth." Grinker states, that "[s]ignificant social, cultural, linguistic, and economic differences have developed between North and South during the past five decades, apart from the ideological divide that never previously existed throughout Korean history."[46] Adopting a confederation may be a way for most Koreans to slowly come to terms with these fissures, eventually allowing them to recover a unified national identity. A confederation may also make the most sense psychologically to both sides. It would reduce fears by the North of being rapidly absorbed into a totally foreign political system, while allowing the South to postpone formal integration until similar economic systems evolve.[47]

Even with a change in the political and social environment, a confederation on the heels of a DPRK collapse still faces several obstacles, to include first establishing a level of political, economic, and social stabilization. In addition, agreement on a confederation is predicated on the assumption that whoever claims leadership of NK will gain legitimacy in the eyes of its populace, and be recognized by the international community. Once this is accomplished, the new leadership must share the same goal as the South in pursuing a confederation, to include working through contentious issues related to previous proposals. In this regard, the ROK may enjoy a degree of leverage, considering the support the new leadership will likely require from the U.N. and the region in order to alleviate the situation.

The success of a confederation would also require the full support of the NEAPSM and its members. While the viewpoint each party would have toward a confederation cannot definitively be determined, some inferences can be made. Based on the discussion above, a confederation in the eyes of China, Russia, and Japan may be appealing. This would allow gradual economic and social reform in the North, as well as give them more time to address the number of issues associated with reunification. In essence, regional members may view a confederation as a "happy medium," given their concerns about what a unified Korea may represent in terms of regional competition. This consideration, combined with the myriad of those discussed, will also have significant implications for U.S. policy choices and interests in the region.

VI. Implications for the U.S.

Security and stability in Northeast Asia are of utmost importance to U.S interests. The most recent National Security Strategy (2006) singles out the DPRK's nuclear program and illicit activities as impediments to peace and stability in the region.[48] Peace and stability provide the U.S. opportunities for economic growth through continued access to Asian markets and valuable resources. Currently, U.S. businesses conduct approximately $700 billion in trade while investing more than $200 billion in the region. Additionally, more than one-third of total U.S. trade is conducted in Northeast Asia and of millions of U.S. jobs rely on continued growth and development in the area.[49] Over the years, the presence of U.S. military forces supported by bilateral security treaties with nations such as South Korea and Japan has prohibited any regional power from gaining hegemonic influence. The collapse of the DPRK presents the U.S. with a major challenge, and if not handled thoughtfully, could upset this equilibrium. Multilateralism offers the U.S. short-term and long-term advantages that the current San Francisco System cannot address.

The initial period following a DPRK collapse is perhaps the most critical, one in which an established multilateral structure will have the greatest impact. The complex issues associated with the development of a regional multilateral framework require prior consensus and planning in order to effectively address the large host of problems and concerns associated with a collapse. How these issues are coordinated and dealt with in the days and weeks following a collapse will impact U.S objectives of peace and stability. If not thoroughly debated multilaterally, any one issue could have ripple effects expanding into a regional crisis. For instance, China's concern for massive refugee flows into Manchuria as well as worries over U.S. intervention above the 38th parallel could prompt the PRC to move ground forces into NK under the guise of regional security.[50] However, this move may be interpreted by Japan, the ROK, and U.S. as offensive, thus potentially pulling the region into a second Korean War. By promoting a multilateral framework, the U.S. can mitigate misperceptions among regional peers by creating an atmosphere of transparency and cooperation. Additionally, multilateral engagement allows the U.S. to balance the burden of stabilizing Korea, at a time when its financial and military resources are stretched thin. The cost of reunifying Korea alone has been estimated at approximately $2-3 trillion, not including political and social costs.[51] Regional cooperation, through humanitarian and energy assistance, will not only help mitigate these costs, but leverage the necessary manpower, allowing the U.S. to uphold its other commitments around the globe.

Conceivably, the greatest advantage of multilateralism is its potential long-term effects. As presented in Section II, while broad multilateral organizations have developed in Southeast Asia, multilateralism in Northeast Asia has been nonexistent. Stabilizing and reforming NK multilaterally may provide the mechanism to build the structure in Northeast Asia for collective security and transparency that has long been absent. A multilateral security framework in Northeast Asia, by itself, may not offer a complete sense of security for the nations involved; however, it may be practical in augmenting the current bilateral alliance system by building assurance and reducing misunderstanding and distrust among those in the region.[52]

The collapse of the DPRK will offer the U.S. a unique opportunity for expanding its current bilateral "hub and spoke" process into a broader multilateral system. As Kent Calder cited the 1950 Korean War and the 1997 Asian Financial Crisis as two "critical junctures" in the evolution of East Asian multilateralism, the collapse of the DPRK may mark a third critical juncture in this development.[53] The U.S. has relied on the "hub and spoke" method to offer stability and ensure its interests in the region. However, the potential that NK may cease to exist or redefine itself as an amenable regional partner, may increase the need for the U.S. to supplement this system. In the particular case of South Korea, the absence of a North Korean threat may call into question the continued viability of a U.S.-ROK security pact, thus eroding the Korean spoke of the wheel. Additionally, the continued use of this bilateral system, in and by itself, may not be enough due to rising nationalism in China, Japan, and Korea. The need for these countries to deal with each other directly on issues related to history and national self-esteem will be greater than ever before.[54] For these reasons, shifting to multilateralism as the primary component of U.S. Northeast Asian policy requires a great deal of understanding of Asian culture. In Europe, this has been comparatively easy due to a considerable degree of common interest and cultural identity. The Europeans, in fact, preferred multilateral institutions virtually from the start, with little cajoling by the U.S.[55] However, in Northeast Asia this commonality has never really established itself as a result of historical divisiveness in the region.

It is difficult to predict the future path Korea would take either unified or as a confederation. This path, as unpredictable as it appears, may impact the design of U.S. forces stationed there in a profound manner. However, due to the large role the U.S. will play in the stabilization and reconciliation processes, the presence of U.S. military forces on the peninsula will probably endure, as it has in Germany for nearly two decades.[56] If and when a post-DPRK multilateral security framework is discussed, the configuration, size, and location of U.S. forces will be a hotly debated topic, particularly with regard to China. China will want to maintain its buffer from the U.S. and likely question the validity of keeping a U.S. military presence in Japan and Korea.[57] Long-term considerations such as this will drive U.S. decision makers to weigh the benefits of promoting multilateralism in conjunction with, or instead of its current bilateral system.

VII. Conclusion/Recommendations

A collapse of the DPRK is arguably one the most feared and greatly anticipated prospects confronting Northeast Asia today. Concerns over a renewed offensive by the North to forcibly reunify the peninsula are slowly being replaced by worries of an economic and social disaster brought on by the disintegration of a starving North. Nested within these issues is the tumultuous history of the region reflected in the regional interests of the ROK, China, Japan, and Russia. For the past half-century, the U.S. has unquestionably acted as a stabilizer and balancer in the region through its use of bilateral agreements and force presence. Consequently, multilateralism in Northeast Asia has traveled an uneven path, making the outlook for establishing an enduring framework a topic of debate.

For these reasons, this paper utilized the collapse of the DPRK as an event that could potentially galvanize support for a regional multilateral structure. This study examined the lack of Northeast Asian multilateralism since the end of WWII, and presented the complexity of achieving success in the midst of diverse interests and views. Additionally, an effort was made to analyze the argument surrounding reunification, and whether a collapse of the DPRK would necessarily make such an outcome a certainty. After presenting a series of short and long-term implications for U.S. interests in the region, three broad recommendations for U.S. policy are offered: (1) initiate early coordination among regional partners in preparing for a collapse, (2) increase U.S. readiness by incorporating multilateral considerations into current theater plans, and (3) promote the establishment of a long-term regional multilateral structure.

1. *Initiate early coordination among regional partners:* Due to the current state of the DPRK, it's plausible that a collapse could occur at any time. While the U.S. and its allies closely monitor indications of instability and impending collapse, the closed nature of the North Korean government precludes any certainty of when and how quickly this could occur. A dialogue among regional powers needs to begin now in order to openly discuss the host of issues associated with a collapse as well as the prospects for developing a regional framework. Admittedly, addressing NK's demise while the DPRK is still intact seems impracticable; however, multilateral meetings on this topic specifically do not necessarily have to take place at this stage. Bilateral discussions between the U.S, ROK, China, Russia, and Japan would be the best early mechanism for initiating a discussion. In particular, the U.S and ROK need to arrive at a mutual understanding regarding ROK goals as they relate to the future of Korea, and be able to articulate that vision to other regional members. It's important the ROK facilitate these discussions in order to validate any proposals as Korean plans and not U.S. plans.

2. *Increase U.S. readiness:* For over fifty years, the U.S. military has maintained a high state of readiness on the Korean peninsula. Combined Forces Command (CFC) reviews contingency plans on a regular basis and exercises them through combined annual training between U.S. and ROK forces. Specifically, the U.S. and ROK typically focus on conventional scenarios largely based on NK aggression. In order to enhance its readiness in responding to a collapse, CFC should expand its contingency plans to reflect a multilateral operating environment. At a minimum, exercises should be expanded to include NK collapse scenarios. This would allow planners to validate any current theater plans related to a DPRK collapse as well as incorporate regional considerations beyond the U.S-ROK alliance. Integrating political, economic, and humanitarian aspects into its existing plans will spur needed coordination among U.S. military, interagency, and allies in order to build the most effective courses of action. This idea is supported by a recent recommendation made by the Council on Foreign Relations (CFR) that state current CFC contingency plans should include a comprehensive interagency assessment that is coordinated by the National Security Council and incorporates input from the Department of State, Department of Treasury, and the Agency for International Development.[58] In addition, injecting multilateral considerations and alternatives into the planning process will not only enable the U.S. to employ its forces more efficiently, but also anticipate regional responses and potential flash points.

3. *Promote a long-term regional multilateral structure:* The collapse of the DPRK provides the U.S. with the window of opportunity to help build a lasting multilateral structure in Northeast Asia. Building on gradual advances in economic integration that have already occurred, the U.S. should promote a structure that addresses the security concerns of all in the region. While a NATO-style security arrangement may not be attainable from the outset, an

already established forum such as the NEAPSM may provide the foundation from which collective security can grow. Nevertheless, traditional methods of promoting peace and security in the region in order to balance or buffer tensions may continue even after a permanent multilateral security framework is developed. Regardless of how and in what form Korean unification eventually occurs, the U.S. will likely continue leveraging the full range of its instruments of power, using bilateral engagement as it deems necessary. However, establishing a permanent multilateral framework in Northeast Asia to supplement, and not replace the current bilateral alliance system, may provide a sense of security and confidence to all.[59] This will help prevent the reemergence of regional rivalries, promote peaceful resolution of differences, thus ensuring continued U.S access to and economic prosperity in the region.

These recommendations by themselves are not intended to be a prescription for success in Northeast Asia, but rather a starting point for more research and study. Diplomatic prowess, military force, or economic strength alone will not guarantee success in a region as complex as Northeast Asia. In the end, real success will be defined by the regional powers surrounding Korea and their ability to overcome centuries of mistrust in order to find common ground suitable to their own interests. While overcoming these obstacles in the midst of a DPRK collapse appears a formidable task, the benefits of multilateralism make the efforts by all those involved a worthwhile endeavor.

Notes

[1] Lewis, Leo. "Kim Jong-Il Being Treated by Brain Surgeon." *Times Online*, 28 October, 2008.

[2] Windrem, Robert. "U.S. Calls Kim Jong Il's Health a 'concern'." *NBC News*, 29 May 2007.

[3] There have been numerous pieces written on possible DPRK implosion scenarios. For the purpose of this paper, the collapse of the DPRK national government was chosen due to its potential "worst case" implications. See Pritchard, Charles L. *Korean Reunification: Implications for the United States and Northeast Asia.* Uri Party Foundation: International Symposium on Peace and Prosperity in Northeast Asia. Washington D.C.: The Brookings Institution, 2005. 4-5.

[4] Stares, Paul B. and Wit, Joel S. *Preparing for a Sudden Change in North Korea.* Council Special Report No. 42. New York, NY: Council on Foreign Relations, Center for Preventive Action, 2009. 22.

[5] Ibid, 3-6.

[6] There are literally hundreds of books about the wars that have taken place in Northeast Asia between the countries mentioned. Throughout history, control of Korea has been at the forefront, widely viewed as a dagger pointed at Japan's heart as well as a bridge to the Asian mainland. See Samuel Hawley, *The Imjin War. Japan's Sixteenth-Century Invasion of Korea and Attempt to Conquer China* and Stephen Turnbull, *Samurai Invasion: Japan's Korean War 1592-98,* as examples.

[7] Calder, Kent E. *East Asian Multilateralism: Prospects for Regional Stability.* Baltimore, MD: The Johns Hopkins University Press, 2008. 18-29.

[8] Ibid, 18. The draft was developed by the U.S. stipulating that the multilateral agreement would be terminated if the U.N. covered the area, or a larger formal framework was created merging with the Pacific Pact.

[9] Ibid, 23. The intervention of the Chinese in Korea instilled fear in U.S. policy makers over the obligation to defend Hong Kong if such a collective security pact were signed.

[10] Ibid. 4. The San Francisco System of bilateral agreements was named after the San Francisco Peace Treaty of 1951 that formally ended the war with Japan. This treaty was signed at the Presidio, and was shortly followed by the U.S.-Japan Mutual Security Treaty.

[11] Ibid, 24.

[12] Ibid, 32-34. The Chiang Mai agreement was an initiative between the ASEAN+3 heads to create a network of bilateral currency swap agreements to prevent any future crisis. Though the agreements were bilateral, the multilateral process used to achieve the agreements represented a substantial advance, particularly in Northeast Asia toward regional cooperation.

[13] *The Newly Emerging Asian Order and the Korean Peninsula.* Joint U.S.–Korea Academic Studies Vol. 15. Washington D.C.: The Korea Economic Institute, 2005. 164.

[14] Ibid, 182-83.

[15] Ibid, 173. Members include the U.S., China, Japan, Russia, South Korea and North Korea.

[16] Tovar, Suzanne M. *How Will External Powers Affect Korean Reunification?* Monterey, CA: Naval Postgraduate School, 2005. 81

[17] *Northeast Asian Security after Korean Reconciliation or Reunification.* IFPA-JIIA Summary Report. Washington D.C.: Institute for Foreign Policy Analysis and Japan Institute of International Affairs, 2002. 10

[18] See Marcus Noland. *The Economic Integration of the Korean Peninsula*, Charles L Pritchard. *Korean Reunification: Implications for the United States and Northeast Asia,* and Yamaji, Hideki. *Policy Recommendations for Japan: Unification of the Korean Peninsula,* as examples.

[19] When Germany reunited, the GDR had a population of 17 million, about a fourth of the FRG's 60 million, compared to the DPRK's 21 million, about half of the ROK's 43 million. See Karlynn Peltz O'Shaughnessy. *The Economic Implications of Korean Reunification.* Carlisle Barracks, PA: U.S Army War College, 2003. 9.

[20] Yamaji, Hideki. *Policy Recommendations for Japan: Unification of the Korean Peninsula.* The Brookings Institute Center for Northeast Asian Policy Studies. Washington D.C.: The Brooking Institution, 2004. 4.

[21] Maxwell, David S. *Catastrophic Collapse of North Korea: Implications for the United States Military.* Fort Leavenworth, KS: School of Advanced Military Studies, 1996. 19.

19

[22] The issue over the status of Korea between the U.S. and Soviet Union was addressed through the Moscow Communique on 27 December 1945. Under this agreement, a U.S.-Soviet Union Joint Commission was established to form a provisional Korean government. See Pak,Chi Young. *Korea and the United Nations.* The Hague, NL: Kluwer Law International, 2000. 3-11.

[23] See Calder and Fukuyama, *East Asian Multilateralism: Prospects for Regional Stability* and Noland and Haggard, *A Security and Peace Mechanism for Northeast Asia.*

[24] The NEAPSM is a working group established in 2007 to address security issues in Northeast Asia beyond the purview of the 6PT. See Noland, Marcus and Stephan Haggard. *A Security and Peace Mechanism for Northeast Asia: The Economic Dimension.* Washington D.C.: Peterson Institute for Economics, 2008. 1.

[25] The five permanent members include the U.S., China, Russia, Britain, and France. See United Nations Website. "UN Charter: Chapter Five," Article 23-32. http://www.un.org/

[26] It's important to remember that in 1950 when the UN invoked Chapter VII and passed UNSCR 82, China's seat on the council was held by the Republic of China (Taiwan) and the Soviet Union was absent.

[27] See Maxwell, *Catastrophic Collapse of North Korea.* 1-9.

[28] Polack, Jonathan D. and Lee, Chung Min. *Preparing for Korean Unification: Scenarios and Implications.* RAND Corporation Special Report. Washington D.C.: The Arroyo Center, 1999. 15.

[29] *A Blueprint for U.S. Policy Toward a Unified Korea.* CSIS Working Group Report. Washington D.C.: Center for Strategic and International Studies, August 2002. 29.

[30] Yamaji, *Policy Recommendations for Japan: The Unification of the Korean Peninsula.* 6-7.

[31] Maxwell, *Catastrophic Collapse of North Korea.* 21.

[32] Ibid, 22.

[33] IFPA-JIIA, *Northeast Asian Security after Korean Reconciliation or Reunification.* 6-7.

[34] Polack, Jonathan D. and Lee, Chung Min. *Preparing for Korean Unification: Scenarios and Implications.* 15-16.

[35] IFPA-JIIA, *Northeast Asian Security after Korean Reconciliation or Reunification.* 6-7.

[36] Taken from "The Unification Policy of the Kim Young Sam Administration," from the Korean Web Weekly Magazine, January 1996. See Maxwell, David S. *Catastrophic Collapse of North Korea: Implications for the United States Military.* Fort Leavenworth, KS: School of Advanced Military Studies, 1996. 18.

[37] See, Nicholas Eberstadt *Hastening Korean Reunification*, Marcus Noland , *Avoiding the Apocalypse: The Future of the Two Koreas,* Pritchard, *Korea Reunification: Implications for the U.S. and Northeast Asia,* and Jonathan Polack and Lee, Chung Min *Preparing for Korean Unification: Scenarios and Implications*, as just a few examples.

[38] Polack, Jonathan D. and Lee, Chung Min. *Preparing for Korean Unification: Scenarios and Implications.* 39-45.

[39] Harrison, Selig. *Korean Endgame: A Strategy for Reunification and U.S. Disengagement.* Princeton, NJ: Princeton University Press, 2002. 74-100.

[40] Pak, *Korea and the United Nations.* 21-22.

[41] Ibid, 75.

[42] NK had previously proposed a confederation in 1960 and again in 1973. The major difference between these two and 1980 was that the earlier proposals were seen as a pit stop on the way to reunification. The 1980 proposal was viewed by the DPRK as a permanent form of a unified state in Korea in order to avoid addressing what a reunified government would look like. See Tae, Hwan Kwak. *The Four Powers and Korean Unification Strategies.* Seoul, Korea: Kyungnam University Press, 1997. 119-121.

[43] The spokesman made the comparison between Hong Kong and China by stating that in a Korean Confederation one side would not revert to the other side as in the case of Hong Kong. See Harrison, *Korean Endgame.* 76-77.

[44] Ibid, 78.

[45] Ibid, 78.

[46] Ibid, 99-100.

[47] Ibid, 100.

[48] The President of the United States. *The National Security Strategy of the United States of America.* Washington, D.C.: The White House, 2006. President, "The National Security Strategy of the United States of America." 26.

[49] CSIS, *A Blueprint for U.S. Policy Toward a Unified Korea.* 15.

[50] In 2004, it was reported China replaced its armed police forces along the China-NK border with an approximately 100,000 regular military troops, suggesting that the inflow of North Korean refugees into China remains a top concern within the PRC government. See Pritchard, *Korean Reunification: Implications for the United States and Northeast Asia.* 7.

[51] Wolf, Charles. *Straddling Economics and Politics: Cross-Cutting Issues in Asia, the United States, and the Global Economy.* RAND Corporation Special Report. Washington D.C.: The Arroyo Center, 2004. 202.

[52] Yamaji, *Policy Recommendations for Japan: Unification of the Korean Peninsula.* 7.

[53] Calder and Fukuyama, *East Asian Multilateralism.* 235-236.

[54] Ibid, 235-236.

[55] Ibid, 241. Fukuyama cites NATO and the EU as two major examples. The NATO treaty was a European initiative preceded by the Brussels Treaty, a multilateral effort without the U.S. in 1948. The EU arose out of the European Coal and Steel Community, an initiative of France, and accepted by the FRG, Italy, and the Benelux.

[56] IFPA-JIIA, *Northeast Asian Security after Korean Reconciliation or Reunification.* 5.

[57] Ibid, 13. According to the IFPA-JIIA, such a scenario may require a renegotiation of the existing U.S-ROK alliance that may involve a major shift in the American force structure on the Peninsula toward air and naval power.

[58] Stares and Wit, *Preparing for Sudden Change in North Korea.* 32.

[59] Yamaji, *Policy Recommendations for Japan: Unification of the Korean Peninsula.* 7.

Bibliography

A Blueprint for U.S. Policy Toward a Unified Korea. CSIS Working Group Report. Washington D.C.: Center for Strategic and International Studies, August 2002.

Calder, Kent E. and Fukayama, Francis. *East Asian Multilateralism: Prospects for Regional Stability.* Baltimore, MD: The Johns Hopkins University Press, 2008.

The Challenges of Reconciliation and Reform in Korea. Joint U.S.–Korea Academic Studies Vol. 12. Washington D.C.: The Korea Economic Institute, 2002.

China: The Balance Sheet: What the World Needs to Know About the Emerging Superpower. CSIS Working Group Report. Washington D.C.: Center for Strategic and International Studies, June 2005.

Eberstadt, Nicholas. *Hastening Korean Reunification.* AEI Report. Washington D.C.: The American Enterprise Institute for Public Policy Research, 2000.

Harrison, Selig. *Korean Endgame: A Strategy for Reunification and U.S. Disengagement.* Princeton, NJ: Princeton University Press, 2002.

Haselden, Carl E. Jr. "The Effects of Korean Unification on the U.S. Military Presence in Northeast Asia." *Parameters*, Winter 2002-2003: 120-130.

Jordan, Matthew J. *Multilateralism in Northeast Asia.* Newport, RI: Naval War College, 2003.

Kwak, Tae Hwan. *The Four Powers and Korean Unification Strategies.* Seoul, Korea: Kyungnam University Press, 1997.

Lee, Hee-Ok. *China's Northeast Asian Project: Political Backgrounds and Implications.* East Asian Review, Vol. 18 No, 4, Winter 2006.

Lewis, Leo. "Kim Jong-Il Being Treated by Brain Surgeon." *Times Online*, 28 October, 2008.

Maxwell, David S. *Catastrophic Collapse of North Korea: Implications for the United States Military.* Fort Leavenworth, KS: School of Advanced Military Studies, 1996.

The National Security Strategy of the United States of America. The President of the United States. Washington, DC: The White House, 2006.

The Newly Emerging Asian Order and the Korean Peninsula. Joint U.S.–Korea Academic Studies Vol. 15. Washington D.C.: The Korea Economic Institute, 2005.

Noland, Marcus. *Avoiding the Apocalypse: The Future of the Two Koreas.* Washington D.C.: Institute for International Economics, 2000.

Noland, Marcus. *Economic Integration of the Korean Peninsula.* Washington D.C.: Institute for
 International Economics, 1998.

Noland, Marcus. *Economic Strategies for Reunification: Korea's Future and the Great
 Powers.* Washington D.C.: The National Bureau of Asian Research in association with
 the University of Washington Press, 2001.

Noland, Marcus and Stephan Haggard. *A Security and Peace Mechanism for Northeast Asia:
 The Economic Dimension.* Washington D.C.: Peterson Institute for Economics, 2008.

Northeast Asian Security after Korean Reconciliation or Reunification. IFPA-JIIA Summary
 Report. Washington D.C.: Institute for Foreign Policy Analysis and Japan Institute of
 International Affairs, 2002.

O'Shaughnessy, Karlynn Peltz COL. *The Economic Implications of Korean Reunification.*
 Carlisle Barracks, PA: U.S Army War College, 2003.

Pak,Chi Young. *Korea and the United Nations.* The Hague, NL: Kluwer Law International,
 2000.

Polack, Jonathan D. and Lee, Chung Min. *Preparing for Korean Unification: Scenarios and
 Implications.* RAND Corporation Special Report. Washington D.C.: The Arroyo Center,
 1999.

Pritchard, Charles L. *Korean Reunification: Implications for the United States and Northeast
 Asia.* Uri Party Foundation: International Symposium on Peace and Prosperity in
 Northeast Asia. Washington D.C.: The Brookings Institution, 2005.

Stares, Paul B. and Wit, Joel S. *Preparing for a Sudden Change in North Korea.* Council
 Special Report No. 42. New York, NY: Council on Foreign Relations, Center for
 Preventive Action, 2009.

Tae, Hwan Kwak. *The Four Powers and Korean Unification Strategies.* Seoul, Korea:
 Kyungnam University Press, 1997.

Tovar, Suzanne M. *How Will External Powers Affect Korean Reunification?* Monterey, CA:
 Naval Postgraduate School, 2005.

UN Charter: Chapter Five. United Nations Website. Article 23-32. http://www.un.org/

Windrem, Robert. "U.S. Calls Kim Jong Il's Health a 'concern'." *NBC News,* 29 May 2007.

Wolf, Charles. *Straddling Economics and Politics: Cross-Cutting Issues in Asia, the United
 States, and the Global Economy.* RAND Corporation Special Report. Washington D.C.:
 The Arroyo Center, 2004.

Yamaji, Hideki. *Policy Recommendations for Japan: Unification of the Korean Peninsula.* The Brookings Institute Center for Northeast Asian Policy Studies. Washington D.C.: The Brooking Institution, 2004.